2ND EDITION

LEVEL **3B**

PIANO
Adventures® *by Nancy and Randall Faber*
THE BASIC PIANO METHOD

FABER
PIANO ADVENTURES®

3042 Creek Drive
Ann Arbor, Michigan 48108

LEVEL 3B TECHNIQUE SECRETS

These four Technique Secrets are used as daily warm-ups for the exercises and pieces in this book.
The teacher should demonstrate each "technique secret" as it is introduced.

1. The first secret is a **CLOSED HAND FOR SCALE PASSAGES**

Exercise: Finger Fireworks

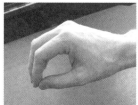

- With palm up, bring your R.H. fingertips and thumb together. Notice your *cupped* hand. Then turn your hand over and look for tall knuckles.

- As you play, check for a tall knuckle on finger 3. Thumb plays *lightly* on the side tip.

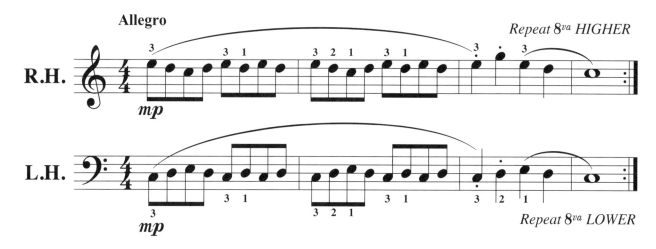

2. The second secret is **THE UP-TOUCH**

Exercise: Finger Springs

From the surface of the key, "spring off" with active fingers and forearm thrust. Use a quick, upward wrist motion.

The up-touch sets the hand in place for the next chord *(preparation)*.

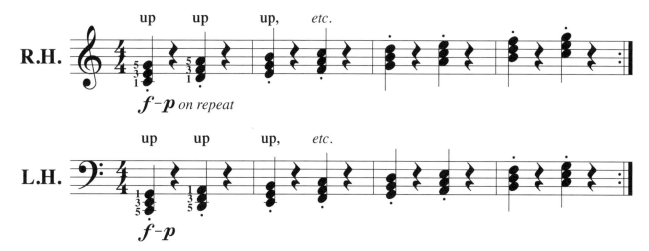

Lesson p.6 (Key of A Minor), Lesson p.7 (Primary Chords in A Minor)
FF1289

3. The third secret is **VOICING THE MELODY**
Exercise: Melody Maker

The melody must "sing" over the *accompaniment*. This is called **voicing the melody**.

• Use arm weight to voice the R.H. melody. Use *less* weight in the L.H. for a softer tone.

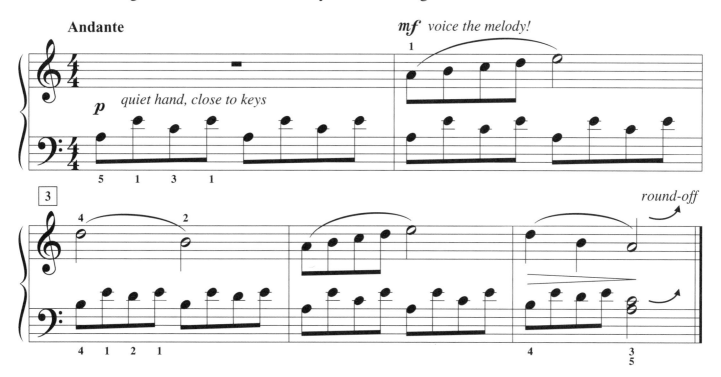

4. The fourth secret is **OPEN HAND FOR EXTENSIONS**
Exercise: Hand Toss

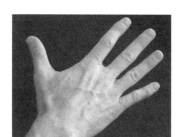

• With both palms down, rapidly close then open your hands (extending fingers 2, 3, 4, and 5) eight times.

• Then play each exercise using a light thumb.

• Continue this pattern UP the white keys on **F**, **G**, **A**, **B**, and **C**.

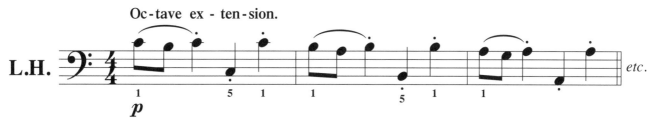

• Continue this pattern DOWN the white keys on **G**, **F**, **E**, **D**, and **C**.

Key of Am

Technique Secret 1:
closed hand for scale passages

Warm-up with *Finger Fireworks* (p. 2).

Rippling Triplets
(for R.H. alone)

- Play the thumb *lightly*, perched on the side tip.

- *Listen* for even triplets that "ripple" up and down the scale.

- Use the metronome goals below. Can you play by memory?

Allegro (♩ = 100-132)

Metronome goals: ♩ = 120 ___   ♩ = 132 ___   You choose: ♩ = ___

Your left hand may not be as fast as your right hand.

- Practice at a slower tempo, gradually increasing your speed.

Rippling Triplets
(for L.H. alone)

Allegro (♩ = 100-132)

Metronome goals: ♩ = 120 ___   ♩ = 132 ___   You choose: ♩ = ___

Technique Secret 2:
the up-touch

Warm-up with *Finger Springs* (p. 2).

• Use an up-touch to spring off the keys
  for the chords in *measures 5-8*.

The Windy Chase
Primary Chord Study in A Minor

With gusto (♩ = 108-120)

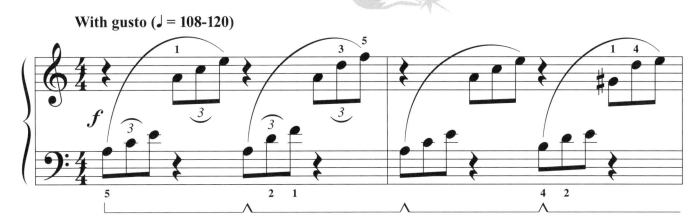

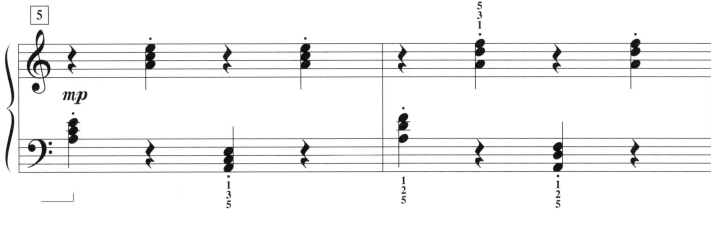

Lesson p.7 (Primary Chords in A Minor)

closed hand for scale passages

Warm-up with *Finger Fireworks* (p. 2).

- Practice the R.H. alone for accurate fingering.
- Next, play *andante*, hands together, observing the dynamics.

Graceful Ski Run

Scale Study in A Minor

Andante (♩ = 76-88)

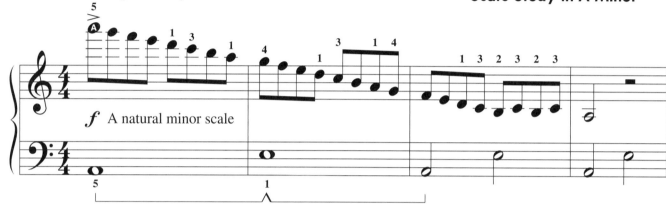

f A natural minor scale

p A harmonic minor scale

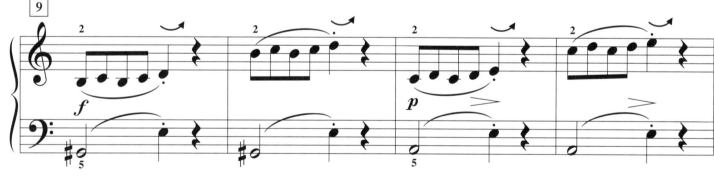

f

p

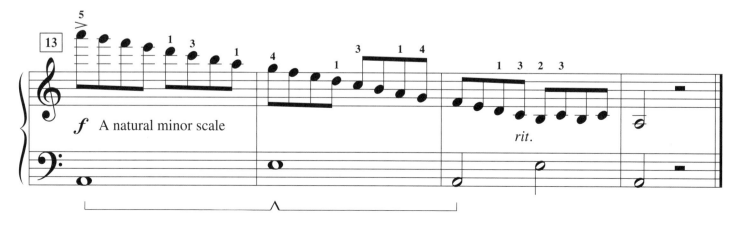

f A natural minor scale

rit.

📖 Lesson pp.8-9 (Energico)   FF128

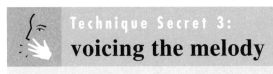

Technique Secret 3:
voicing the melody

Warm-up with *Melody Maker* (p. 3).

Bel Canto means "beautiful singing." Imagine—

- Your R.H. is the singer. Use arm weight for an expressive, warm tone.
- Your L.H. is a soft guitar. Play with *light* fingers, close to the keys.

Bel Canto

Study in Balance in A Minor

A pianist who performs with artistry can play a melody expressively with the left hand.

For expressive balance between the hands:

- Make the **L.H. melody** "sing" by playing to the bottom of the key, using the weight of the arm.

- Play the **R.H. chords** softly, close to the keys. Use a gentle *up-touch*.

Nightfall

Key of _____ Minor

Rather slowly, with expression (♩ = 80-92)

N. Faber

📖 Lesson pp.12-13 (Snowfall)

FF1289

F1289

- Shape the scales with *crescendos* and *diminuendos*. Play with a closed, cupped hand.

- Can you play these exercises by memory?

Em Racecar Scales

(for R.H. alone)

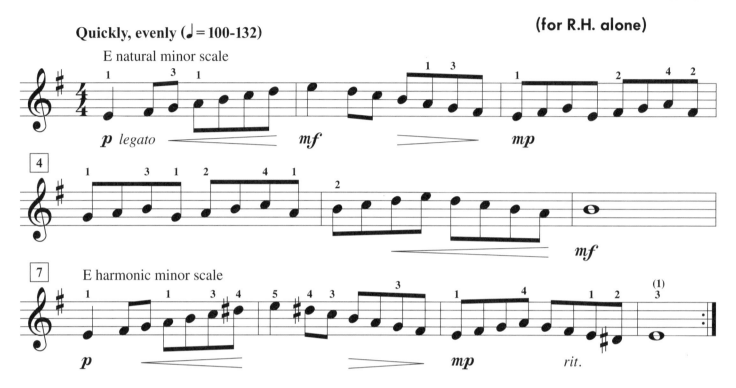

Em Racecar Scales

(for L.H. alone)

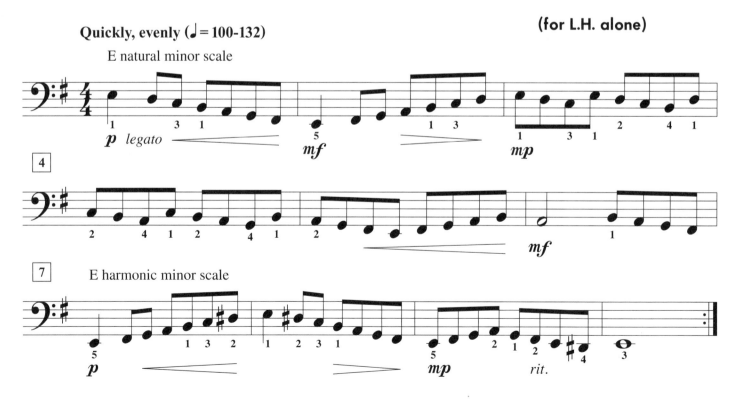

- Notice the rhythm progresses from **quarter notes**, to **8th notes**, and back to **quarter notes**. The beat must always be steady as the rhythms change.

- Use energetic *staccatos* for the quarter note chords. Play the 8th notes close to the keys with precise rhythm.

Rhythm Expo

E Minor Primary Chord Study

       📖 Lesson p.15 (Primary Chords in E Minor)

- For smooth **cross-hand arpeggios**, begin crossing the L.H. over while the R.H. is still playing.

- Listen for clean pedal changes.

The Gathering Storm

Key of _____ Major/Minor

N. Faber

Allegro moderato (♩ = 100-120)

🎵 Lesson pp.16-17 (Sea Chantey)

FF128

Technique Secret 1:
closed hand for scale passages

Warm-up with *Finger Fireworks* in **D minor** (p. 2).

Dm Racecar Scales
(for R.H. alone)

Quickly, evenly (♩ = 100-132)

D natural minor scale

D harmonic minor scale

Teacher Duet: (Student plays *1 octave higher*. Teacher pedals.)

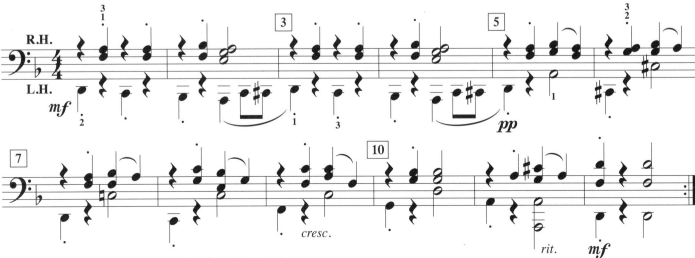

📖 Lesson pp.22-23 (Primary Chords in D Minor)

FF128

Your left hand may require more practice for building speed.

- Play slowly to build your L.H. finger coordination.

- Then play a little faster, giving musical shape by observing the dynamics.

Dm Racecar Scales

(for L.H. alone)

Lesson pp.22-23 (Primary Chords in D Minor)

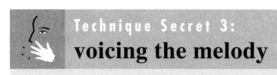

Technique Secret 3:
voicing the melody

Warm-up with *Melody Maker* in **D minor** (p. 3).

Harmony Check: Write **i**, **iv**, or **V7** in the boxes.

Magic Carpet Variations

Primary Chords in D Minor

- When you can easily play the Theme, learn
  Variation 1 and Variation 2 for more practice
  with **i**, **iv**, and **V7** chords.

VARIATION 1: Waltz bass pattern

- Complete **Variation 1** by playing *measures 9-14* on page 16.

VARIATION 2: Broken chord pattern

- Complete **Variation 2** by playing *measures 9-14* on page 16.

A pianist with artistry can change **articulations** easily.
This study alternates frequently between

- **R.H. slurred notes**
- **interlocking staccato passages**

• Stay close to the keys for the *staccato* measures.
  Listen for rhythmic precision between the hands!

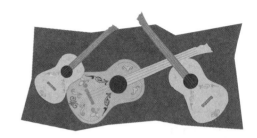

Guitars of Seville

Articulation Study in D Minor

Mauro Giuliani
(1781-1829, Italy)
adapted

Allegro moderato (♩ = 84-108)

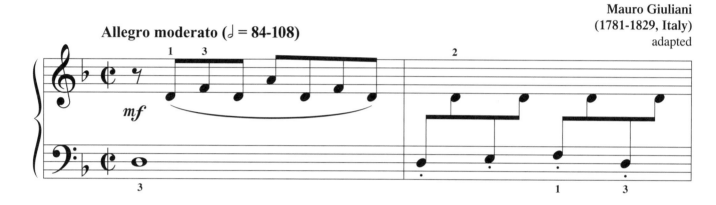

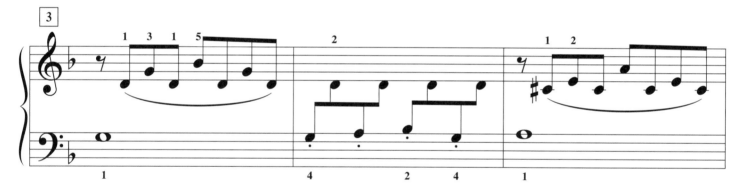

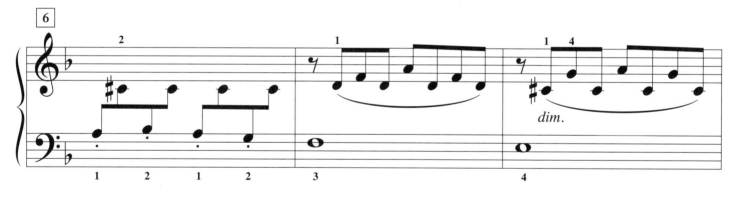

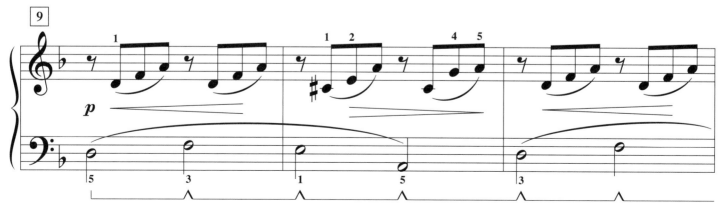

📖 Lesson pp.27-29 (Legend of Madrid)   FF128

 Technique Secret 4:

open hand for extensions

Warm-up with *Hand Toss* (p. 3).

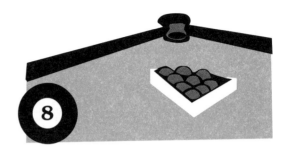

8

- First play the L.H. alone. Remember the F♯ and C♯ from the key signature.

L.H. Octave Bounce

With a steady beat (♩ = 112-132)

f - *p* on repeat

5

- Transpose to **C major**.

- First play the R.H. alone.
  Did you remember the F♯ and C♯?

R.H. Octave Bounce

With a steady beat (♩ = 112-132)

f - *p* on repeat

5

- Transpose to **G major**.

20   Lesson p.30 (The Scale in Octaves)

FF128

- Notice the s-l-o-w tempo—*lento*. Play the broken octaves gracefully. Let your wrist rise gently to a *light* thumb.

- Create drama with all the dynamic marks.

The Faraway Castle
Pedal Study with Broken Octaves

Henri Bertini
(1798-1876, France)
original form*

*Op. 137, No. 22, Prelude

Lesson pp.32-33 (Phantom of the Keys)

One-Octave Arpeggio Review

Play this example using a circular *"under and over"* motion of the wrist.* The wrist moves laterally (sideways) to transfer arm weight from finger to finger.

- Use the "wrist circle" technique for the opening phrase.

- Play to the bottom of the key using **arm weight** to create a deep, rich melody.

Loxodonta Africana
(African Elephant)

N. Faber

*introduced in the Level 3A Lesson Book, page 60

*Omit the top note of these chords if the student cannot reach an octave.

TRI▲D

- Practice these major triads going up *chromatically*.
- "Cushion" each chord with a small down-up "wrist bow."

The 12 Major Triads

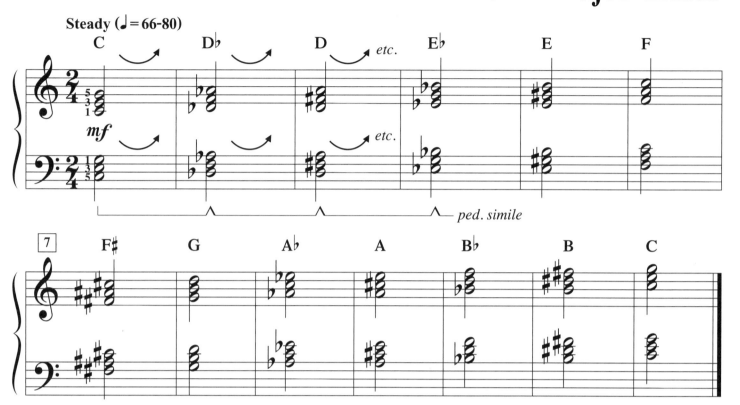

- For smooth hand crossings, *prepare* the next chord while the other hand is still playing.

Andante Triad Study

Blocked/Broken Major Chords

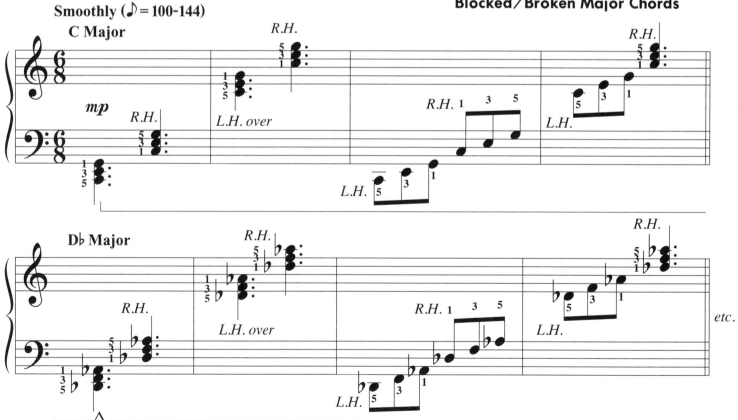

- Continue this pattern going UP chromatically (**D**, **E♭**, **E**, **F**, **F♯**, **G**, **A♭**, **A**, **B♭**, **B**, and **C**).

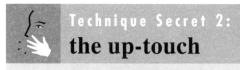

Technique Secret 2:
the up-touch

Warm-up with *Finger Springs* (p. 2).

For L.H., think *down* on beat 1
and *up-touch* on beats 3 and 4.

Syncopated Triads

R.H. Study with Blocked Major Triads

- Continue this pattern going UP chromatically (**F♯**, **G**, **A♭**, **A**, **B♭**, **B**, and **C**).

L.H. Variation (Root and 5th)

Extra Credit: Play *Syncopated Triads* using this variation in the bass.

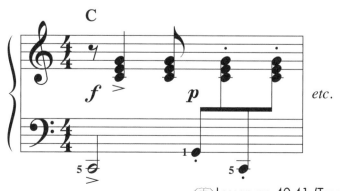

Lesson pp.40-41 (Tropical Island)   25

Technique Secret 4:
open hand for extensions

Warm-up with *Hand Toss* (p. 3).

- Use a circular motion for the **one-octave arpeggio**. Let your hand close as you complete the circle.

- For the L.H. chords, use an up-touch for the staccato and arm weight on the accent.

Arpeggio Whirl
Wrist Circle Study

Moderately (♩ = 69-88)

- Continue this pattern going UP chromatically (E♭, E, F, F♯, G, A♭, etc.).

Lesson pp.42-43 (Liebestraum)

FF128

- Practice these minor triads going up *chromatically*.
- "Cushion" each chord with a small down-up "wrist bow."

The 12 Minor Triads

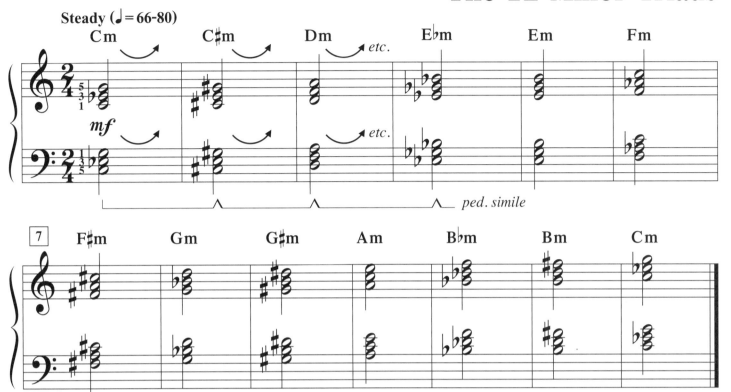

Technique Secret 3:
voicing the melody

Warm-up with *Melody Maker* (p. 3).

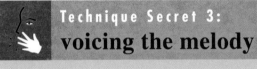

Minor Serenade

Study in Voicing and Phrasing

- Continue this pattern going UP chromatically (**Dm, E♭m, Em, Fm, F♯m, Gm, G♯m,** etc.).

Lesson pp.42-43 (Liebestraum)

Warm-up with *Finger Springs* (p. 2).

Use the "spring" of the up-touch to *prepare* the **L.H. octave shifts**. Each spring carries the hand in an *arc* to the next triad.

Minor Triad Jumps
Preparation Study

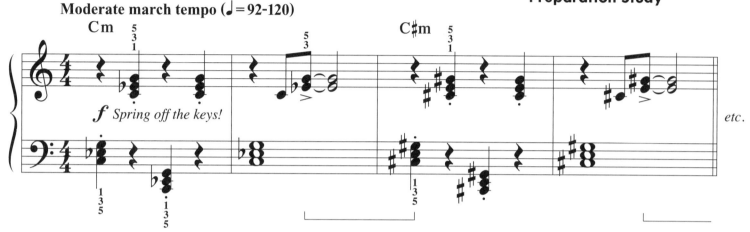

• Continue this pattern going UP chromatically (**Dm, E♭m, Em, Fm, F♯m**, etc.).

Major/Minor Waves
Broken Chord Study with One-Octave Arpeggios

• Continue this pattern going UP chromatically (**D♭, D, E♭, E, F, F♯**, etc.).

- Play with deep tone, shaping each phrase with an expressive diminuendo.

Adagio in Blue
Octave Study Across the Keys

Technique Hint:

Toss your R.H. thumb into each accented note.
This back-and-forth tossing (or rocking) motion is
called *rotation**. Fingers 5 and 2 stay close to the keys.

1st Inversion Toss
Blocked and Broken
(for R.H. alone)

Fast, lightly (♩ = 100-120)

• Continue this white key pattern UP beginning on **B**, **C**, **D**, and **E**.

Technique Hint:

Toss L.H. finger 5 into each accented note using
rotation. Fingers 1 and 3 stay close to the keys.

1st Inversion Toss
Blocked and Broken
(for L.H. alone)

Fast, lightly (♩ = 100-120)

• Continue this white key pattern UP beginning on **B**, **C**, **D**, and **E**.

*introduced in Level 3A *Technique & Artistry*, page 3

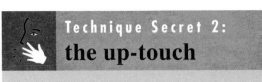

Fifties Serenade

Preparation with 1st Inversions

Hand Position for Inversions

To play inversions, open the hand by extending between the *thumb* and *finger 2*. Fingers 2, 3, 4, 5 stay together.

Sunrise

Major Triad Inversion Study

- Transpose this **major** chord inversion exercise to three other major keys. You choose!

____ major   ____ major   ____ major

Technique Secret 2:
the up-touch

Warm-up with *Finger Springs* (p. 2).

Two-Hand Tango

Minor Triad Inversion Study

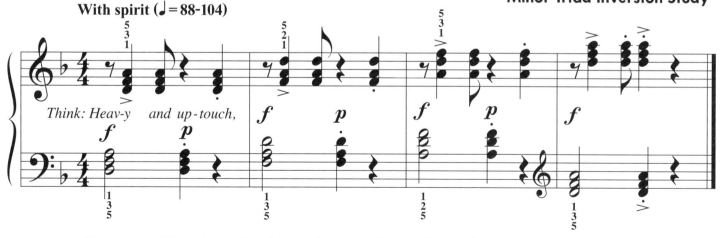

- Transpose this **minor** chord inversion exercise to three other minor keys. You choose!

____ minor   ____ minor   ____ minor

Lesson pp.52-53 (Swing Low, Sweet Chariot)   FF1289

This piece is written entirely for the **L.H. alone**.
The L.H. must play both *melody* and *harmony* notes.
Contrast *forte* and *piano* touches for "two tiers" of sound.

Campfire Guitar

Inversion Etude for L.H. Alone

Lesson pp.52-53 (Swing Low, Sweet Chariot)

Technique Secret 1:

closed hand for scale passages

Warm-up with *Finger Fireworks* (p. 2).

- Practice these patterns until they are easy.

- Can you build speed using the metronome goals below?

Jigsaw Puzzle

16th-Note Rhythms

Rhythm Pattern:

Steady (♩ = 72-92)

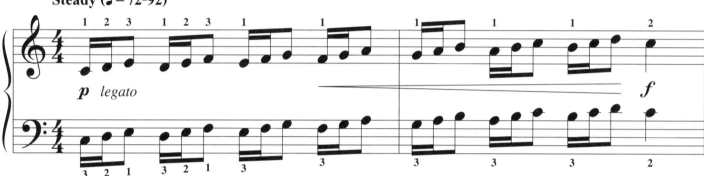

Rhythm Pattern:

Steady (♩ = 72-92)

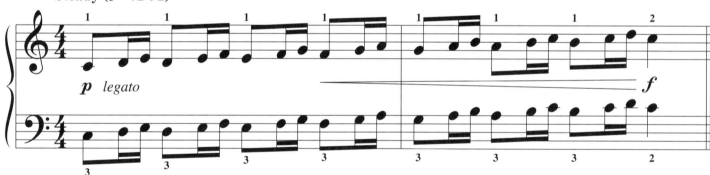

Rhythm Pattern:

Steady (♩ = 72-92)

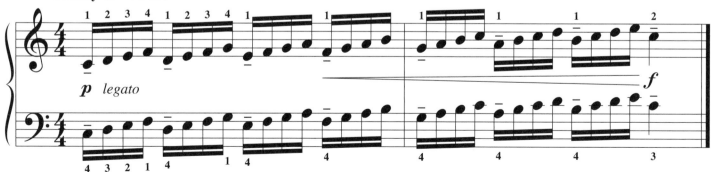

_____ ♩ = 72 *Andante*   _____ ♩ = 80 *Moderato*   _____ ♩ = 92 *Allegro*

Technique Secret 2:

the up-touch

Warm-up with *Finger Springs* (p. 2).

Scale Journey

**16th-Note Scale Study
Key of A Minor**

- Practice the R.H. alone, shaping each scale.
  Practice the L.H. alone using a gentle up-touch.

- Build speed using the metronome goals below.
  Then transpose to C major!

Allegretto (♩ = 72-92)

_____ ♩ = 72 *Andante*   _____ ♩ = 80 *Moderato*   _____ ♩ = 92 *Allegro*

FF1289

📖 Lesson pp.56-57 (Adagio and Allegro)   35

closed hand for scale passages

Warm-up with *Finger Fireworks* (p. 2).

Rhythm Venture

Study in 8ths, Triplets, and 16th Notes
Key of D Major

Ferdinand Beyer
(1803-1863, Germany)
adapted

- Set your tempo based on how comfortably you can play the 16th notes at *measures 5-6*.

Moderato (♩ = 63-88)

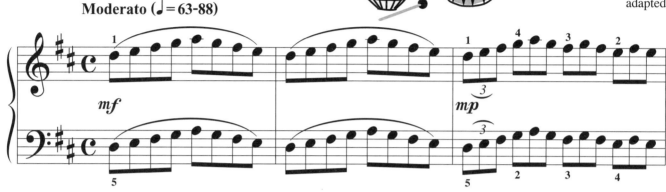

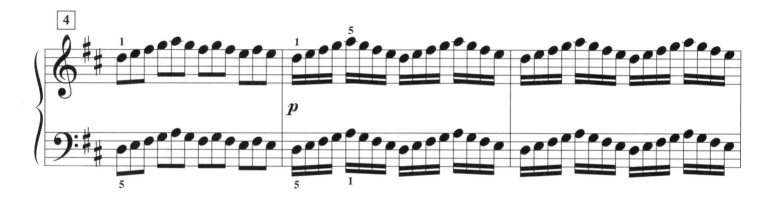

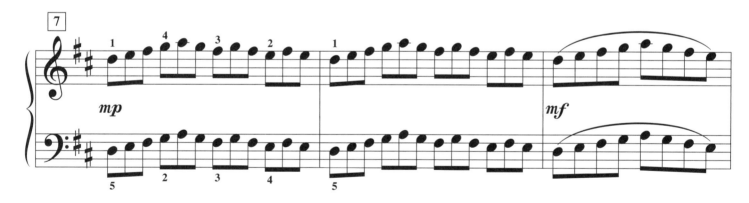

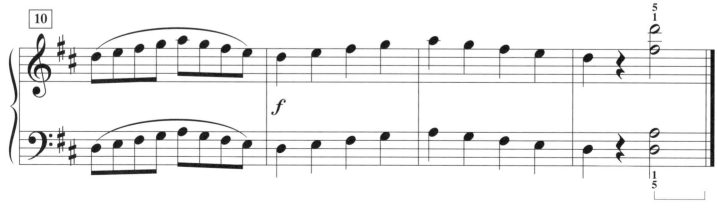

*from Elementary Instruction Book for the Pianoforte, Op. 101, No. 86, originally in the key of C.

Technique Secret 2:
the up-touch

Warm-up with *Finger Springs* (p. 2).

- Hint: Be careful to "sneak" into the first note of each L.H. scale. No accents!

Czerny's Allegro

Study in L.H. Scale Passages

Carl Czerny
(1791-1857, Austria)
original form*

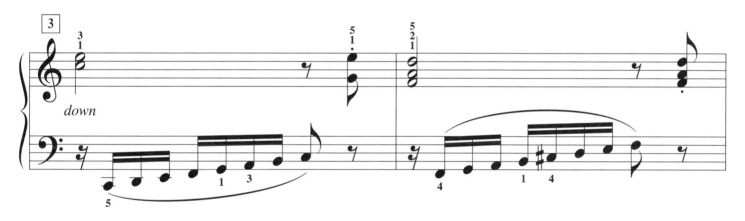

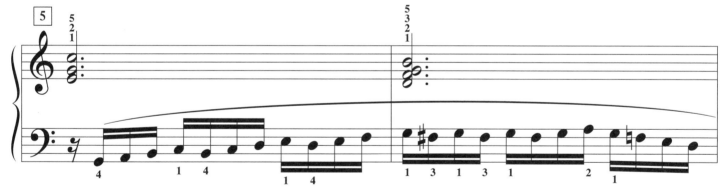

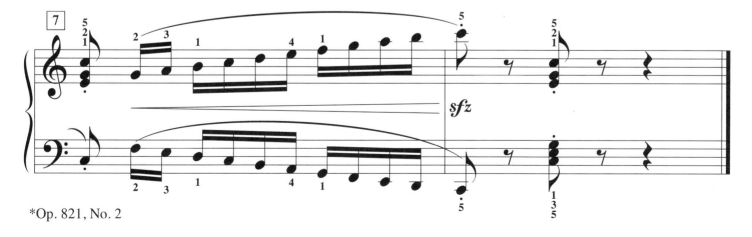

*Op. 821, No. 2

This piece reviews the following **technique** and **artistry** concepts.
Can you include each in your playing?

- closed hand for scale passages
- open hand for extensions
- the up-touch
- balance between the hands
- voicing the melody
- changing articulations

Enjoy your fine technique and artistry!

Rondoletto

Key of ____ Major/Minor

Christian Traugott Brunner
(1792-1874, Germany)
original form

Allegretto (♩ = 72-108)

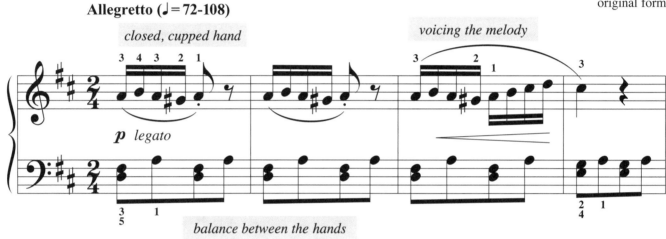

closed, cupped hand

voicing the melody

balance between the hands

open hand for extensions

Lesson pp.60-63 (Pachelbel Canon)   FF1281

Certificate
of Achievement

CONGRATULATIONS TO

_____

(Your name)

You have completed

PIANO ADVENTURES®

Technique & Artistry Book **LEVEL 3B**

and are now ready for

PIANO ADVENTURES®

Technique & Artistry Book **LEVEL 4**

Keep up the amazing work!

Teacher: _____

Date: _____